Autumnal
Tints

Autumnal Tints

Henry David Thoreau

APPLEWOOD BOOKS
BEDFORD, MASSACHUSETTS

Autumnal Tints was originally published in the October, 1862 *Atlantic Monthly*.

Cover art: "Near the Village, October," by George Inness. Reprinted by permission of the Cincinnati Art Museum. Gift of Emilie L. Heine in memory of Mr. and Mrs. John Hauck.

ISBN 1-55709-442-X

Thank you for purchasing an Applewood Book Applewood reprints America's lively classics— books from the past that are of interest to modern readers. For a free copy of our current catalog, write to: Applewood Books, Box 365, Bedford, MA 01730.

Library of Congress Cataloging-in-Publication Data
Thoreau, Henry David, 1817-1862.
Autumnal tints / by Henry David Thoreau.
p.   cm.
"Autumnal tints was first published in the October 1862 Atlantic monthly"—T.p. verso.
ISBN 1-55709-442-X
1. Natural history—New England.   2. Autumn—New England.   3. Fall foliage—New England.   I. Title
QH104.5.N4T49   1996
508.74–dc20   96-21109
CIP

EUROPEANS coming to America are surprised by the brilliancy of our autumnal
foliage. There is no account of such a
phenomenon in English poetry, because the
trees acquire but few bright colors there. The
most that Thomson says on this subject in his
"Autumn" is contained in the lines,—

"But see the fading many-colored woods,
  Shade deepening over shade, the country round
  Imbrown; a crowded umbrage, dusk and dun,
  Of every hue, from wan declining green to sooty dark":-

and in the line in which he speaks of

"Autumn beaming o'er the yellow woods."

The autumnal change of our woods has not
made a deep impression on our own literature
yet. October has hardly tinged our poetry.

A great many, who have spent their lives in
cities, and have never chanced to come into
the country at this season, have never seen this,
the flower, or rather the ripe fruit, of the year. I
remember riding with one such citizen, who,

though a fortnight too late for the most brilliant tints, was taken by surprise, and would not believe that there had been any brighter. He had never heard of this phenomenon before. Not only many in our towns have never witnessed it, but it is scarcely remembered by the majority from year to year.

Most appear to confound changed leaves with withered ones, as if they were to confound ripe apples with rotten ones. I think that the change to some higher color in a leaf is an evidence that it has arrived at a late and perfect maturity, answering to the maturity of fruits. It is generally the lowest and oldest leaves which change first. But as the perfect winged and usually bright-colored insect is short-lived, so the leaves ripen but to fall.

Generally, every fruit, on ripening, and just before it falls, when it commences a more independent and individual existence, requiring less nourishment from any source, and that not so much from the earth through its stem as from the sun and air, acquires a bright tint. So do leaves. The physiologist says it is "due to an increased absorption of oxygen." That is the scientific account of the matter,—

only a reassertion of the fact. But I am more interested in the rosy cheek than I am to know what particular diet the maiden fed on. The very forest and herbage, the pellicle of the earth, must acquire a bright color, an evidence of its ripeness,—as if the globe itself were a fruit on its stem, with ever a cheek toward the sun.

Flowers are but colored leaves, fruits but ripe ones. The edible part of most fruits is, as the physiologist says, "the parenchyma or fleshy tissue of the leaf," of which they are formed.

Our appetites have commonly confined our views of ripeness and its phenomena, color, mellowness, and perfectness, to the fruits which we eat, and we are wont to forget that an immense harvest which we do not eat, hardly use at all, is annually ripened by Nature. At our annual Cattle Shows and Horticultural Exhibitions, we make, as we think, a great show of fair fruits, destined, however, to a rather ignoble end, fruits not valued for their beauty chiefly. But round about and within our towns there is annually another show of fruits, on an infinitely

grander scale, fruits which address our taste
for beauty alone.

October is the month for painted leaves.
Their rich glow now flashes round the world.
As fruits and leaves and the day itself acquire a
bright tint just before they fall, so the year near
its setting. October is its sunset sky; November
the later twilight.

I formerly thought that it would be worth
the while to get a specimen leaf from each
changing tree, shrub, and herbaceous plant,
when it had acquired its brightest characteris-
tic color, in its transition from the green to the
brown state, outline it, and copy its color
exactly, with paint in a book, which should be
entitled, *"October, or Autumnal Tints"*;—
beginning with the earliest reddening,—
Woodbine and the lake of radical leaves, and
coming down through the Maples, Hickories,
and Sumachs, and many beautifully freckled
leaves less generally known, to the latest Oaks
and Aspens. What a memento such a book
would be! You would need only to turn over
its leaves to take a ramble through the
autumn woods whenever you pleased. Or if I
could preserve the leaves themselves, unfad-

ed, it would be better still. I have made but little progress toward such a book, but I have
endeavored, instead, to describe all these
bright tints in the order in which they present
themselves. The following are some extracts
from my notes.

THE PURPLE GRASSES.

By the twentieth of August, everywhere in
woods and swamps, we are reminded of the
fall, both by the richly spotted Sarsaparilla-
leaves and Brakes, and the withering and
blackened Skunk-Cabbage and Hellebore,
and, by the river-side, the already blackening
Pontederia.

The Purple Grass (*Eragròstis pectinàcea*) is
now in the height of its beauty. I remember
still when I first noticed this grass particularly. Standing on a hillside near our river, I saw,
thirty or forty rods off, a stripe of purple half a
dozen rods long, under the edge of a wood,
where the ground sloped toward a meadow. It
was as high-colored and interesting, though
not quite so bright, as the patches of Rhexia,

being a darker purple, like a berry's stain laid on close and thick. On going to and examining it, I found it to be a kind of grass in bloom, hardly a foot high, with but few green blades, and a fine spreading panicle of purple flowers, a shallow, purplish mist trembling around me. Close at hand it appeared but a dull purple, and made little impression on the eye; it was even difficult to detect; and if you plucked a single plant, you were surprised to find how thin it was, and how little color it had. But viewed at a distance in a favorable light, it was of a fine lively purple, flower-like, enriching the earth. Such puny causes combine to produce these decided effects. I was the more surprised and charmed because grass is commonly of a sober and humble color.

With its beautiful purple blush it reminds me, and supplies the place, of the Rhexia, which is now leaving off, and it is one of the most interesting phenomena of August. The finest patches of it grow on waste strips or selvages of land at the base of dry hills, just above the edge of the meadows, where the greedy mower does not deign to swing his scythe; for this is a thin and poor grass, beneath his notice. Or, it may be, because it is so beautiful he does not know that it exists; for the same eye does not see this and Timothy. He carefully gets the meadow hay and the more nutritious grasses which grow next to that, but he leaves this fine purple mist for the walker's harvest,—fodder for his fancy stock. Higher up the hill, perchance, grow also Black-berries, John's-Wort, and neglected, withered, and wiry June-Grass. How fortunate that it grows in such places, and not in the midst of the rank grasses which are annually cut! Nature thus keeps use and beauty distinct. I know many such localities, where it does not fail to present itself annually, and paint the earth with its blush. It grows on the gentle slopes, either in a continuous patch or in scattered and rounded tufts a foot in diameter, and it lasts till it is killed by the first smart frosts.

In most plants the corolla or calyx is the part which attains the highest color, and is the most attractive; in many it is the seed-vessel or fruit; in others, as the Red Maple, the leaves; and in others still it is the very culm itself which is the principal flower or blooming part.

The last is especially the case with the Poke or Garget (*Phytolacca decándra*). Some which stand under our cliffs quite dazzle me with their purple stems now and early in September. They are as interesting to me as most flowers, and one of the most important fruits of our autumn. Every part is flower, (or fruit,) such is its superfluity of color,—stem, branch, peduncle, pedicel, petiole, and even the at length yellowish purple-veined leaves. Its cylindrical racemes of berries of various hues, from green to dark purple, six or seven inches long, are gracefully drooping on all sides, offering repasts to the birds; and even the sepals from which the birds have picked the berries are a brilliant lake-red, with crimson flame-like reflections, equal to anything of the kind,—all on fire with ripeness. Hence the *lacca*, from *lac*, lake. There are at the same time flower-buds, flowers, green berries, dark purple or ripe ones, and these flower-like sepals, all on the same plant.

We love to see any redness in the vegetation of the temperate zone. It is the color of colors. This plant speaks to our blood. It asks a bright sun on it to make it show to best

advantage, and it must be seen at this season
of the year. On warm hillsides its stems are
ripe by the twenty-third of August. At that
date I walked through a beautiful grove of
them, six or seven feet high, on the side of
one of our cliffs, where they ripen early. Quite
to the ground they were a deep brilliant purple with a bloom, contrasting with the still
clear green leaves. It appears a rare triumph of
Nature to have produced and perfected such a
plant, as if this were enough for a summer.
What a perfect maturity it arrives at! It is the
emblem of a successful life concluded by a
death not premature, which is an ornament
to Nature. What if we were to mature as perfectly, root and branch, glowing in the midst
of our decay, like the Poke! I confess that it
excites me to behold them. I cut one for a
cane, for I would fain handle and lean on it. I
love to press the berries between my fingers,
and see their juice staining my hand. To walk
amid these upright, branching casks of purple
wine, which retain and diffuse a sunset glow,
tasting each one with your eye, instead of
counting the pipes on a London dock, what a
privilege! For Nature's vintage is not confined

to the vine. Our poets have sung of wine, the product of a foreign plant which commonly they never saw, as if our own plants had no juice in them more than the singers. Indeed, this has been called by some the American Grape, and though a native of America, its juices are used in some foreign countries to improve the color of the wine; so that the poetaster may be celebrating the virtues of the Poke without knowing it. Here are berries enough to paint afresh the western sky, and play the bacchanal with, if you will. And what flutes its ensanguined stems would make, to be used in such a dance! It is truly a royal plant. I could spend the evening of the year musing amid the Poke-stems. And perchance amid these groves might arise at last a new school of philosophy or poetry. It lasts all through September.

At the same time with this, or near the end of August, a to me very interesting genus of grasses, Andropogons, or Beard-Grasses, is in its prime. *Andropogon furcatus*, Forked Beard-Grass, or call it Purple-Fingered Grass; *Andropogon scoparius*, Purple Wood-Grass; and *Andropogon* (now called *Sorghum*) *nutans*,

Indian-Grass. The first is a very tall and slender-culmed grass, three to seven feet high, with four or five purple finger-like spikes raying upward from the top. The second is also quite slender, growing in tufts two feet high by one wide, with culms often somewhat curving, which, as the spikes go out of bloom, have a whitish fuzzy look. These two are prevailing grasses at this season on dry and sandy fields and hillsides. The culms of both, not to mention their pretty flowers, reflect a purple tinge, and help to declare the ripeness of the year. Perhaps I have the more sympathy with them because they are despised by the farmer, and occupy sterile and neglected soil. They are high-colored, like ripe grapes, and express a maturity which the spring did not suggest. Only the August sun could have thus burnished these culms and leaves. The farmer has long since done his upland haying, and he will not condescend to bring his scythe to where these slender wild grasses have at length flowered thinly; you often see spaces of bare sand amid them. But I walk encouraged between the tufts of Purple Wood-Grass, over the sandy fields, and along the edge of the

Shrub-Oaks, glad to recognize these simple contemporaries. With thoughts cutting a broad swathe I "get" them, with horse-raking thoughts I gather them into windrows. The fine-eared poet may hear the whetting of my scythe. These two were almost the first grasses that I learned to distinguish, for I had not known by how many friends I was surrounded,—I had seen them simply as grasses standing. The purple of their culms also excites me like that of the Poke-Weed stems.

Think what refuge there is for one, before August is over, from college commencements and society that isolates! I can skulk amid the tufts of Purple Wood-Grass on the borders of the "Great Fields." Wherever I walk these afternoons, the Purple-Fingered Grass also stands like a guide-board, and points my thoughts to more poetic paths than they have lately travelled.

A man shall perhaps rush by and trample down plants as high as his head, and cannot be said to know that they exist, though he may have cut many tons of them, littered his stables with them, and fed them to his cattle for years. Yet, if he ever favorably attends to them, he may be overcome by their beauty. Each humblest plant, or weed, as we call it, stands there to express some thought or mood of ours; and yet how long it stands in vain! I had walked over those Great Fields so many Augusts, and never yet distinctly recognized these purple companions that I had there. I had brushed against them and trodden on them, forsooth; and now, at last, they, as it were, rose up and blessed me. Beauty and true wealth are always thus cheap and despised. Heaven might be defined as the place which men avoid. Who can doubt that these grasses, which the farmer says are of no account to him, find some compensation in your appreciation of them? I may say that I never saw them before,—though, when I came to look them face to face, there did come down to me a purple gleam from previous years; and now, wherever I go, I see hardly anything else. It is the reign and presidency of the Andropogons.

Almost the very sands confess the ripening influence of the August sun, and methinks, together with the slender grasses waving over them, reflect a purple tinge. The impurpled sands! Such is the consequence of all this sunshine absorbed into the pores of plants and of the earth. All sap or blood is now wine-colored. At last we have not only the purple sea, but the purple land.

The Chestnut Beard-Grass, Indian-Grass, or Wood-Grass, growing here and there in waste places, but more rare than the former, (from two to four or five feet high,) is still handsomer and of more vivid colors than its congeners, and might well have caught the Indian's eye. It has a long, narrow, one-sided, and slightly nodding panicle of bright purple and yellow flowers, like a banner raised above its reedy leaves. These bright standards are now advanced on the distant hill-sides, not in large armies, but in scattered troops or single file, like the red men. They stand thus fair and bright, representative of the race which they are named after, but for the most part unobserved as they. The expression of this grass haunted me for a week, after I first passed and noticed it, like the glance of an eye. It stands like an Indian chief taking a last look at his favorite hunting-grounds.

THE RED MAPLE.

By the twenty-fifth of September, the Red Maples generally are beginning to be ripe. Some large ones have been conspicuously changing for a week, and some single trees are now very brilliant. I notice a small one, half a mile off across a meadow, against the green wood-side there, a far brighter red than the blossoms of any tree in summer, and more conspicuous. I have observed this tree for several autumns invariably changing earlier than its fellows, just as one tree ripens its fruit earlier than another. It might serve to mark the season, perhaps. I should be sorry, if it were cut down. I know of two or three such trees in different parts of our town, which might, perhaps, be propagated from, as early ripeners or September trees, and their seed be advertised in the market, as well as that of radishes, if we cared as much about them.

At present these burning bushes stand chiefly along the edge of the meadows or I distinguish them afar on the hillsides here and

there. Sometimes you will see many small
ones in a swamp turned quite crimson when
all other trees around are still perfectly green,
and the former appear so much the brighter
for it. They take you by surprise, as you are
going by on one side, across the fields, thus
early in the season, as if it were some gay
encampment of the red men, or other
foresters, of whose arrival you had not heard.

Some single trees, wholly bright scarlet,
seen against others of their kind still freshly
green, or against evergreens, are more memorable than whole groves will be by-and-by.
How beautiful, when a whole tree is like one
great scarlet fruit full of ripe juices, every leaf,
from lowest limb to topmost spire, all aglow,
especially if you look toward the sun! What
more remarkable object can there be in the
landscape? Visible for miles, too fair to be
believed. If such a phenomenon occurred but
once, it would be handed down by tradition to
posterity, and get into the mythology at last.

The whole tree thus ripening in advance
of its fellows attains a singular preëminence,
and sometimes maintains it for a week or two.
I am thrilled at the sight of it, bearing aloft its

scarlet standard for the regiment of green-clad foresters around, and I go half a mile out of my way to examine it. A single tree becomes thus the crowning beauty of some meadowy vale, and the expression of the whole surrounding forest is at once more spirited for it.

A small Red Maple has grown, perchance, far away at the head of some retired valley, a mile from any road, unobserved. It has faithfully discharged the duties of a Maple there, all winter and summer, neglected none of its economies, but added to its stature in the virtue which belongs to a Maple, by a steady growth for so many months, never having gone gadding abroad, and is nearer heaven than it was in the spring. It has faithfully husbanded its sap, and afforded a shelter to the wandering bird, has long since ripened its seeds and committed them to the winds, and has the satisfaction of knowing, perhaps, that a thousand little well-behaved Maples are already settled in life somewhere. It deserves well of Mapledom. Its leaves have been asking it from time to time, in a whisper, "When shall we redden?" And now, in this month of September, this month of travelling, when men are hastening to the sea-side, or the mountains, or the lakes, this modest Maple, still without budging an inch, travels in its reputation,—runs up its scarlet flag on that hillside, which shows that it has finished its summer's work before all other trees, and withdraws from the contest. At the eleventh hour of the year, the tree which no scrutiny could have detected here when it was most industrious is thus, by the tint of its maturity, by its very blushes, revealed at last to the careless and distant traveler, and leads his thoughts away from the dusty road into those brave solitudes which it inhabits. It flashes out conspicuous with all the virtue and beauty of a Maple,—*Acer rubrum*. We may now read its title, or *rubric*, clear. Its *virtues*, not its sins, are as scarlet.

Notwithstanding the Red Maple is the most intense scarlet of any of our trees, the Sugar-Maple has been the most celebrated, and Michaux in his "Sylva" does not speak of the autumnal color of the former. About the second of October, these trees, both large and small, are most brilliant, though many are still green. In "sprout-lands" they seem to vie with

one another, and ever some particular one in
the midst of the crowd will be of a peculiarly
pure scarlet, and by its more intense color
attract our eye even at a distance, and carry off
the palm. A large Red-Maple swamp, when at
the height of its change, is the most obviously
brilliant of all tangible things, where I dwell,
so abundant is this tree with us. It varies much
both in form and color. A great many are
merely yellow, more scarlet, others scarlet
deepening into crimson, more red than common. Look at yonder swamp of Maples mixed
with Pines, at the base of a Pine-clad hill, a
quarter of a mile off, so that you get the full
effect of the bright colors, without detecting
the imperfections of the leaves, and see their
yellow, scarlet, and crimson fires, of all tints,
mingled and contrasted with the green. Some
Maples are yet green, only yellow or crimson-
tipped on the edges of their flakes, like the
edges of a Hazel-Nut burr; some are wholly
brilliant scarlet, raying out regularly and finely every way, bilaterally, like the veins of a leaf;
others, of more irregular form, when I turn my
head slightly, emptying out some of its earthiness and concealing the trunk of the tree,

seem to rest heavily flake on flake, like yellow and scarlet clouds, wreath upon wreath, or like snowdrifts driving through the air, stratified by the wind. It adds greatly to the beauty of such a swamp at this season, that, even though there may be no other trees interspersed, it is not seen as a simple mass of color, but, different trees being of different colors and hues, the outline of each crescent tree-top is distinct, and where one laps on to another. Yet a painter would hardly venture to make them thus distinct a quarter of a mile off.

As I go across a meadow directly toward a low rising ground this bright afternoon, I see, some fifty rods off toward the sun, the top of a Maple swamp just appearing over the sheeny russet edge of the hill, a stripe apparently twenty rods long by ten feet deep, of the most intensely brilliant scarlet, orange, and yellow, equal to any flowers or fruits, or any tints ever painted. As I advance, lowering the edge of the hill which makes the firm foreground or lower frame of the picture, the depth of the brilliant grove revealed steadily increases, suggesting that the whole of the inclosed valley is filled with such color. One wonders that the tithing-men and fathers of the town are not out to see what the trees mean by their high colors and exuberance of spirits, fearing that some mischief is brewing. I do not see what the Puritans did at this season, when the Maples blaze out in scarlet. They certainly could not have worshipped in groves then. Perhaps that is what they built meeting-houses and fenced them round with horse-sheds for.

 THE ELM.

Now, too, the first of October, or later, the Elms are at the height of their autumnal beauty, great brownish-yellow masses, warm from their September oven, hanging over the highway. Their leaves are perfectly ripe. I wonder if there is any answering ripeness in the lives of the men who live beneath them. As I look down our street, which is lined with them, they remind me both by their form and color of yellowing sheaves of grain, as if the harvest had indeed come to the village itself, and we might expect to find some maturity and *flavor* in the thoughts of the villagers at last. Under those bright rustling yellow piles just ready to fall on the heads of the walkers, how can any crudity or greenness of thought or act prevail? When I stand where half a dozen large Elms droop over a house, it is as if I stood within a ripe pumpkin-rind, and I feel as mellow as if I were the pulp, though I may be somewhat stringy and seedy withal. What is the late greenness of the English Elm, like a cucumber out of season, which does not know when to have done, compared with the early and golden maturity of the American tree? The street is the scene of a great harvest-home. It would be worth the while to set out these trees, if only for their autumnal value. Think of these great yellow canopies or parasols held over our heads and houses by the mile together, making the village all one and compact,—an *ulmarium*, which is at the same time a nursery of men! And then how gently and unobserved they drop their burden and let in the sun when it is wanted, their leaves not heard when they fall on our roofs and in our streets: and thus the village parasol is shut up and put away! I see the market-man driving into the village, and disappearing under its canopy of Elm-tops, with *his* crop, as into a great granary or barn-yard. I am tempted to go thither as to a husking of thoughts, now dry and ripe, and ready to be separated from their integuments; but, alas! I foresee that it will be chiefly husks and little thought, blasted pig-corn, fit only for cob-meal,— for, as you sow, so shall you reap.

❧ Fallen Leaves. ❧

By the sixth of October the leaves generally begin to fall, in successive showers, after frost or rain; but the principal leaf-harvest, the acme of the *Fall*, is commonly about the six-teenth. Some morning at that date there is perhaps a harder frost than we have seen, and ice formed under the pump, and now, when the morning wind rises, the leaves come down in denser showers than ever. They sud-denly form thick beds or carpets on the ground, in this gentle air, or even without wind, just the size and form of the tree above. Some trees, as small Hickories, appear to have dropped their leaves instantaneously, as a soldier grounds arms at a signal; and those of the Hickory, being bright yellow still, though withered, reflect a blaze of light from the ground where they lie. Down they have come on all sides, at the first earnest touch of autumn's wand, making a sound like rain.

Or else it is after moist and rainy weather that we notice how great a fall of leaves there has been in the night, though it may not yet be the touch that loosens the Rock-Maple leaf. The streets are thickly strewn with the trophies, and fallen Elm-leaves make a dark brown pavement under our feet. After some remarkably warm Indian-summer day or days, I perceive that it is the unusual heat which, more than anything, causes the leaves to fall, there having been, perhaps, no frost nor rain for some time. The intense heat suddenly ripens and wilts them, just as it softens and ripens peaches and other fruits, and causes them to drop.

The leaves of late Red Maples, still bright, strew the earth, often crimson-spotted on a yellow ground, like some wild apples,—though they preserve these bright colors on the ground but a day or two, espe-

cially if it rains. On causeways I go by trees
here and there all bare and smoke-like, having lost their brilliant clothing; but there it
lies, nearly as bright as ever, on the ground on
one side, and making nearly as regular a fig-
ure as lately on the tree. I would rather say
that I first observe the trees thus flat on the
ground like a permanent colored shadow, and
they suggest to look for the boughs that bore
them. A queen might be proud to walk where
these gallant trees have spread their bright
cloaks in the mud. I see wagons roll over
them as a shadow or a reflection, and the dri-
vers heed them just as little as they did their
shadows before.

Birds'-nests, in the Huckleberry and other
shrubs, and in trees, are already being filled
with the withered leaves. So many have fall-
en in the woods, that a squirrel cannot run
after a falling nut without being heard. Boys
are raking them in the streets, if only for the
pleasure of dealing with such clean crisp substances. Some sweep the paths scrupulously
neat, and then stand to see the next breath
strew them with new trophies. The swamp-
floor is thickly covered, and the *Lycopodium*

lucidulum looks suddenly greener amid them. In dense woods they half-cover pools that are three or four rods long. The other day I could hardly find a well-known spring, and even suspected that it had dried up, for it was completely concealed by freshly fallen leaves; and when I swept them aside and revealed it, it was like striking the earth, with Aaron's rod, for a new spring. Wet grounds about the edges of swamps look dry with them. At one swamp, where I was surveying, thinking to step on a leafy shore from a rail, I got into the water more than a foot deep.

When I go to the river the day after the principal fall of leaves, the sixteenth, I find my boat all covered, bottom and seats, with the leaves of the Golden Willow under which it is moored, and I set sail with a cargo of them rustling under my feet. If I empty it, it will be full again to-morrow. I do not regard them as litter, to be swept out, but accept them as suitable straw or matting for the bottom of my carriage. When I turn up into the mouth of the Assabet, which is wooded, large fleets of leaves are floating on its surface, as it were getting out to sea, with room to tack; but next the shore, a little farther up, they are thicker than foam, quite concealing the water for a rod in width, under and amid the Alders, Button-Bushes, and Maples, still perfectly light and dry, with fibre unrelaxed; and at a rocky bend where they are met and stopped by the morning wind, they sometimes form a broad and dense crescent quite across the river. When I turn my prow that way, and the wave which it makes strikes them, list what a pleasant rustling from these dry substances grating on one another! Often it is their undulation only which reveals the water beneath them. Also every motion of the wood-turtle on the shore is betrayed by their rustling there. Or even in mid-channel, when the wind rises, I hear them blown with a rustling sound. Higher up they are slowly moving round and round in some great eddy which the river makes, as that at the "Leaning Hemlocks," where the water is deep, and the current is wearing into the bank.

Perchance, in the afternoon of such a day, when the water is perfectly calm and full of reflections, I paddle gently down the main stream, and, turning up the Assabet, reach a quiet cove, where I unexpectedly find myself surrounded by myriads of leaves, like fellow-voyagers, which seem to have the same purpose, or want of purpose, with myself. See this great fleet of scattered leaf-boats which we paddle amid, in this smooth river-bay, each one curled up on every side by the sun's skill, each nerve a stiff spruce-knee,—like boats of hide, and of all patterns, Charon's boat probably among the rest, and some with lofty prows and poops, like the stately vessels of the ancients, scarcely moving in the sluggish current,—like the great fleets, the dense Chinese cities of boats, with which you mingle on entering some great mart, some New York or Canton, which we are all steadily approaching together. How gently each has been deposited on the water! No violence has been used towards them yet, though, perchance, palpitating hearts were present at the launching. And painted ducks, too, the splendid wood-duck among the rest, often come to sail and float amid the painted leaves,—barks of a nobler model still!

What wholesome herb-drinks are to be had in the swamps now! What strong medicinal, but rich, scents from the decaying

leaves! The rain falling on the freshly dried
herbs and leaves, and filling the pools and
ditches into which they have dropped thus
clean and rigid, will soon convert them into
tea,—green, black, brown, and yellow teas, of
all degrees of strength, enough to set all
Nature a gossiping. Whether we drink them
or not, as yet, before their strength is drawn,
these leaves, dried on great Nature's coppers,
are of such various pure and delicate tints as
might make the fame of Oriental teas.

How they are mixed up, of all species,
Oak and Maple and Chestnut and Birch! But
Nature is not cluttered with them; she is a
perfect husbandman; she stores them all.
Consider what a vast crop is thus annually
shed on the earth! This, more than any mere
grain or seed, is the great harvest of the year.
The trees are now repaying the earth with
interest what they have taken from it. They
are discounting. They are about to add a leaf's
thickness to the depth of the soil. This is the
beautiful way in which Nature gets her muck,
while I chaffer with this man and that, who
talks to me about sulphur and the cost of cart-
ing. We are all the richer for their decay. I am
more interested in this crop than in the

English grass alone or in the corn. It prepares the virgin mould for future cornfields and forests, on which the earth fattens. It keeps our homestead in good heart.

For beautiful variety no crop can be compared with this. Here is not merely the plain yellow of the grains, but nearly all the colors that we know, the brightest blue not excepted: the early blushing Maple, the Poison-Sumach blazing its sins as scarlet, the mulberry Ash, the rich chrome-yellow of the Poplars, the brilliant red Huckleberry, with which the hills' backs are painted, like those of sheep. The frost touches them, and, with the slightest breath of returning day or jarring of earth's axle, see in what showers they come floating down! The ground is all party-colored with them. But they still live in the soil, whose fertility and bulk they increase, and in the forests that spring from it. They stoop to rise, to mount higher in coming years, by subtle chemistry, climbing by the sap in the trees, and the sapling's first fruits thus shed, transmuted at last, may adorn its crown, when, in after-years, it has become the monarch of the forest.

It is pleasant to walk over the beds of these fresh, crisp, and rustling leaves. How beautifully

they go to their graves! how gently lay themselves down and turn to mould!—painted of a
thousand hues, and fit to make the beds of us
living. So they troop to their last resting-
place, light and frisky. They put on no weeds,
but merrily they go scampering over the
earth, selecting the spot, choosing a lot,
ordering no iron fence, whispering all
through the woods about it,—some choosing
the spot where the bodies of men are moul-
dering beneath, and meeting them half-way.
How many flutterings before they rest quietly
in their graves! They that soared so loftily,
how contentedly they return to dust again,
and are laid low, resigned to lie and decay at
the foot of the tree, and afford nourishment to
new generations of their kind, as well as to
flutter on high! They teach us how to die.
One wonders if the time will ever come when
men, with their boasted faith in immortality,
will lie down as gracefully and as ripe,—with
such an Indian-summer serenity will shed
their bodies, as they do their hair and nails.

When the leaves fall, the whole earth is a
cemetery pleasant to walk in. I love to wander
and muse over them in their graves. Here are

no lying nor vain epitaphs. What though you own no lot at Mount Auburn? Your lot is sure-ly cast somewhere in this vast cemetery, which has been consecrated from of old. You need attend no auction to secure a place. There is room enough here. The Loose-strife shall bloom and the Huckleberry-bird sing over your bones. The woodman and hunter shall be your sextons, and the children shall tread upon the borders as much as they will. Let us walk in the cemetery of the leaves,— this is your true Greenwood Cemetery.

THE SUGAR-MAPLE.

But think not that the splendor of the year is over; for as one leaf does not make a summer, neither does one falling leaf make an autumn. The smallest Sugar-Maples in our streets make a great show as early as the fifth of October, more than any other trees there. As I look up the Main Street, they appear like painted screens standing before the houses; yet many are green. But now, or generally by the seventeenth of October, when almost all

Red Maples, and some White Maples, are bare, the large Sugar-Maples also are in their glory, glowing with yellow and red, and show unexpectedly bright and delicate tints. They are remarkable for the contrast they often afford of deep blushing red on one half and green on the other. They become at length dense masses of rich yellow with a deep scarlet blush, or more than blush, on the exposed surfaces. They are the brightest trees now in the street.

The large ones on our Common are particularly beautiful. A delicate, but warmer than golden yellow is now the prevailing color, with scarlet cheeks. Yet, standing on the east side of the Common just before sundown, when the western light is transmitted through them, I see that their yellow even, compared with the pale lemon of an Elm close by, amounts to a scarlet, without noticing the bright scarlet portions. Generally, they are great regular oval masses of yellow and scarlet. All the sunny warmth of the season, the Indian-summer, seems to be absorbed in their leaves. The lowest and inmost leaves next the bole are, as usual, of the most delicate yellow and green, like the complexion of young men brought up in the house. There is an auction on the Common to-day, but its red flag is hard to be discerned amid this blaze of color.

Little did the fathers of the town antici-pate this brilliant success, when they caused to be imported from farther in the country some straight poles with their tops cut off, which they called Sugar-Maples; and, as I remember, after they were set out, a neigh-boring merchant's clerk, by way of jest, plant-ed beans about them. Those which were then jestingly called bean-poles are to-day far the most beautiful objects noticeable in our streets. They are worth all and more than they have cost,—though one of the select-men, while setting them out, took the cold which occasioned his death,—if only because they have filled the open eyes of children with their rich color unstintedly so many Octobers. We will not ask them to yield us so fair a prospect in the autumn. Wealth in-doors may be the inheritance of few, but it is equally distributed on the Common. All chil-dren alike can revel in this golden harvest.

Surely trees should be set in our streets
with a view to their October splendor; though
I doubt whether this is ever considered by the
"Tree Society." Do you not think it will make
some odds to these children that they were
brought up under the Maples? Hundreds of
eyes are steadily drinking in this color, and by
these teachers even the truants are caught
and educated the moment they step abroad.
Indeed, neither the truant nor the studious is
at present taught color in the schools. These
are instead of the bright colors in the apothe-
caries' shops and city windows. It is a pity that
we have no more *Red* Maples, and some
Hickories, in our streets as well. Our paint-
box is very imperfectly filled. Instead of, or
beside, supplying such paint-boxes as we do,
we might supply these natural colors to the
young. Where else will they study color under
greater advantages? What School of Design
can vie with this? Think how much the eyes
of painters of all kinds, and of manufacturers
of cloth and paper, and paper-stainers, and
countless others, are to be educated by these
autumnal colors. The stationer's envelopes
may be of very various tints, yet, not so vari-

ous as those of the leaves of a single tree. If you want a different shade or tint of a particular color, you have only to look farther within or without the tree or the wood. These leaves are not many dipped in one dye, as at the dye-house, but they are dyed in light of infinitely various degrees of strength, and left to set and dry there.

Shall the names of so many of our colors continue to be derived from those of obscure foreign localities, as Naples yellow, Prussian blue, raw Sienna, burnt Umber, Gamboge?—(surely the Tyrian purple must have faded by this time),—or from comparatively trivial articles of commerce,—chocolate, lemon, coffee, cinnamon, claret?—(shall we compare our Hickory to a lemon, or a lemon to a Hickory?)—or from ores and oxides which few ever see? Shall we so often, when describing to our neighbors the color of something we have seen, refer them, not to some natural object in our neighborhood, but perchance to a bit of earth fetched from the other side of the planet, which possibly they may find at the apothecary's, but which probably neither they nor we ever saw? Have we not an *earth*

under our feet,—ay, and a sky over our heads?
Or is the last *all* ultramarine? What do we
know of sapphire, amethyst, emerald, ruby,
amber, and the like,—most of us who take
these names in vain? Leave these precious
words to cabinet-keepers, virtuosos, and
maids-of-honor,—to the Nabobs, Begums,
and Chobdars of Hindostan, or wherever else.
I do not see why, since America and her
autumn woods have been discovered, our
leaves should not compete with the precious
stones in giving names to colors; and, indeed,
I believe that in course of time the names of
some of our trees and shrubs, as well as flowers, will get into our popular chromatic
nomenclature.

But of much more importance than a
knowledge of the names and distinctions of
color is the joy and exhilaration which these
colored leaves excite. Already these brilliant
trees throughout the street, without any
more variety, are at least equal to an annual
festival and holiday, or a week of such. These
are cheap and innocent gala-days, celebrated
by one and all without the aid of committees
or marshals, such a show as may safely be

licensed, not attracting gamblers or rum-sellers, not requiring any special police to keep the peace. And poor indeed must be that New-England village's October which has not the Maple in its streets. This October festival costs no powder, nor ringing of bells, but every tree is a living liberty-pole on which a thousand bright flags are waving.

No wonder that we must have our annual Cattle-Show, and Fall Training, and perhaps Cornwallis, our September Courts, and the like. Nature herself holds her annual fair in October, not only in the streets, but in every hollow and on every hill-side. When lately we looked into that Red-Maple swamp all ablaze, where the trees were clothed in their vestures of most dazzling tints, did it not suggest a thousand gypsies beneath,—a race capable of wild delight,—or even the fabled fawns, satyrs, and wood-nymphs come back to earth? Or was it only a congregation of wearied wood-choppers, or of proprietors come to inspect their lots, that we thought of? Or earlier still, when we paddled on the river through that fine-grained September air, did there not appear to be something new going on under the sparkling surface of the stream, a shaking of props, at least, so that we made haste in order to be up in time? Did not the rows of yellowing Willows and Button-Bushes on each side seem like rows of booths, under which, perhaps, some fluviatile egg-pop equally yellow was effervescing? Did not all these suggest that man's spirits should rise as high as Nature's,—should hang out their flag, and the routine of his life be interrupted by an analogous expression of joy and hilarity?

No annual training or muster of soldiery, no celebration with its scarfs and banners, could import into the town a hundredth part of the annual splendor of our October. We have only to set the trees, or let them stand, and Nature will find the colored drapery,— flags of all her nations, some of whose private signals hardly the botanist can read,—while we walk under the triumphal arches of the Elms. Leave it to Nature to appoint the days, whether the same as in neighboring States or not, and let the clergy read her proclamations, if they can understand them. Behold what a brilliant drapery is her Woodbine flag! What public-spirited merchant, think you, has contributed this part of the show? There is no handsomer shingling and paint than this vine, at present covering a whole side of some houses. I do not believe that the Ivy *never sere* is comparable to it. No wonder it has been extensively introduced into London. Let us have a good many Maples and Hickories and Scarlet Oaks, then, I say. Blaze away! Shall that dirty roll of bunting in the gun-house be all the colors a village can display? A village is not complete, unless it have these trees to mark the season in it. They are important, like the town-clock. A village that has them not will not be found to work well. It has a screw loose, an essential part is wanting. Let us have Willows for spring, Elms for summer, Maples and Walnuts and Tupeloes for autumn, Evergreens for winter, and Oaks for all seasons. What is a gallery in a house to a gallery in the streets, which every market-man rides through, whether he will or not? Of course, there is not a picture-gallery in the country which would be worth so much to us as is the western view at sunset under the Elms of our main street. They are the frame to a picture which is daily painted behind them.

An avenue of Elms as large as our largest and three miles long would seem to lead to some admirable place, though only Concord were at the end of it.

A village needs these innocent stimulants of bright and cheering prospects to keep off melancholy and superstition. Show me two villages, one empowered in trees and blazing with all the glories of October, the other a merely trivial and treeless waste, or with only a single tree or two for suicides, and I shall be sure that in the latter will be found the most starved and bigoted religionists and the most desperate drinkers. Every washtub and milkcan and gravestone will be exposed. The inhabitants will disappear abruptly behind their barns and houses, like desert Arabs amid their rocks, and I shall look to see spears in their hands. They will be ready to accept the most barren and forlorn doctrine,—as that the world is speedily coming to an end, or has already got to it, or that they themselves are turned wrong side outward. They will perchance crack their dry joints at one another and call it a spiritual communication.

But to confine ourselves to the Maples. What if we were to take half as much pains in protecting them as we do in setting them out,—not stupidly tie our horses to our dahlia-stems?

What meant the fathers by establishing this *perfectly living* institution before the church,—this institution which needs no repairing nor repainting, which is continually enlarged and repaired by its growth? Surely they

"Wrought in a sad sincerity;
  Themselves from God they could not free;
  They *planted* better than they knew;—
  The conscious *trees* to beauty grew."

Verily these Maples are cheap preachers, permanently settled, which preach their half-century, and century, ay, and century-and-a-half sermons, with constantly increasing unction and influence, ministering to many generations of men; and the least we can do is to supply them with suitable colleagues as they grow infirm.

✳ THE SCARLET OAK. ✳

Belonging to a genus which is remarkable for the beautiful form of its leaves, I suspect that some Scarlet-Oak leaves surpass those of all other Oaks in the rich and wild beauty of their outlines. I judge from an acquaintance with twelve species, and from drawings which I have seen of many others.

Stand under this tree and see how finely its leaves are cut against the sky,--as it were, only a few sharp points extending from a mid-rib. They look like double, treble, or quadruple crosses. They are far more ethereal than the less deeply scolloped Oak-leaves. They have so little leafy *terra firma* that they appear melting away in the light, and scarcely obstruct our view. The leaves of very young plants are, like those of full-grown Oaks of other species, more entire, simple, and lump-ish in their outlines; but these, raised high on old trees, have solved the leafy problem. Lifted higher and higher, and sublimated more and more, putting off some earthiness and cultivating more intimacy with the light each year, they have at length the least possible amount of earthy matter, and the greatest spread and grasp of skyey influences. There they dance, arm in arm with the light,—tripping it on fantastic points, fit partners in those aërial halls. So intimately mingled are they with it, that, what with their slenderness and their glossy surfaces, you can hardly tell at last what in the dance is leaf and what is light. And when no zephyr stirs, they are at most but a rich tracery to the forest-windows.

I am again struck with their beauty, when, a month later, they thickly strew the ground in the woods, piled one upon another under my feet. They are then brown above, but purple beneath. With their narrow lobes and their bold deep scollops reaching almost to the middle, they suggest that the material must be cheap, or else there has been a lavish expense in their creation, as if so much had been cut out. Or else they seem to us the remnants of the stuff out of which leaves have been cut with a die. Indeed, when they lie thus one upon another, they remind me of a pile of scrap-tin.

Or bring one home, and study it closely at your leisure, by the fireside. It is a type, not from any Oxford font, not in the Basque nor the arrow-headed character, not found on the Rosetta Stone, but destined to be copied in sculpture one day, if they ever get to whittling stone here. What a wild and pleasing outline, a combination of graceful curves and angles! The eye rests with equal delight on what is not leaf and on what is leaf,—on the broad, free, open sinuses, and on the long, sharp, bristle-pointed lobes. A simple oval outline would include it all, if you connected the points of the leaf; but how much richer is it than that, with its half-dozen deep scollops, in which the eye and thought of the beholder are embayed! If I were a drawing master, I would set my pupils to copying these leaves, that they might learn to draw firmly and gracefully.

Regarded as water, it is like a pond with half a dozen broad rounded promontories extending nearly to its middle, half from each side, while its watery bays extend far inland, like sharp friths, at each of whose heads several fine streams empty in,—almost a leafy archipelago.

But it oftener suggests land, and, as
Dionysius and Pliny compared the form of the
Morea to that of the leaf of the Oriental
Plane-tree, so this leaf reminds me of some
fair wild island in the ocean, whose extensive
coast, alternate rounded bays with smooth
strands, and sharp-pointed rocky capes, mark
it as fitted for the habitation of man, and destined to become a centre of civilization at last.
To the sailor's eye, it is a much-indented
shore. Is it not, in fact, a shore to the aërial
ocean, on which the windy surf beats? At
sight of this leaf we are all mariners,—if not
vikings, buccaneers, and filibusters. Both our
love of repose and our spirit of adventure are
addressed. In our most casual glance, perchance, we think, that, if we succeed in doub-
ling those sharp capes, we shall find deep,
smooth, and secure havens in the ample bays.
How different from the White-Oak leaf, with
its rounded headlands, on which no light-
house need be placed! That is an England,
with its long civil history, that may be read.
This is some still unsettled New-found Island
or Celebes. Shall we go and be rajahs there?

By the twenty-sixth of October the large
Scarlet Oaks are in their prime, when other

Oaks are usually withered. They have been kindling their fires for a week past, and now generally burst into a blaze. This alone of *our* indigenous deciduous trees, (excepting the Dogwood, of which I do not know half a dozen, and they are but large bushes) is now in its glory. The two Aspens and the Sugar-Maple come nearest to it in date, but they have lost the greater part of their leaves. Of evergreens, only the Pitch-Pine is still commonly bright.

But it requires a particular alertness, if not devotion to these phenomena, to appreciate the wide-spread, but late and unexpected glory of the Scarlet Oaks. I do not speak here of the small trees and shrubs, which are commonly observed, and which are now withered, but of the large trees. Most go in and shut their doors, thinking that bleak and colorless November has already come, when some of the most brilliant and memorable colors are not yet lit.

This very perfect and vigorous one, about forty feet high, standing in an open pasture, which was quite glossy green on the twelfth, is now, the twenty-sixth, completely changed to bright dark scarlet,—every leaf, between you and the sun, as if it had been dipped into a scarlet dye. The whole tree is much like a heart in form, as well as color. Was not this worth waiting for? Little did you think, ten days ago, that that cold green tree would assume such color as this. Its leaves are still firmly attached, while those of other trees are falling around it. It seems to say,—"I am the last to blush, but I blush deeper than any of ye. I bring up the rear in my red coat. We Scarlet ones, alone of Oaks, have not given up the fight."

The sap is now, and even far into November, frequently flowing fast in these trees, as in Maples in the spring; and apparently their bright tints, now that most other Oaks are withered, are connected with this phenomenon. They are full of life. It has a pleasantly astringent, acorn-like taste, this strong Oak-wine, as I find on tapping them with my knife.

Looking across this woodland valley, a quarter of a mile wide, how rich those Scarlet Oaks, embosomed in Pines, their bright red branches intimately intermingled with them! They have their full effect there. The Pine-boughs are the green calyx to their red petals. Or, as we go along a road in the woods, the sun striking end-wise through it, and lighting up the red tents of the Oaks, which on each side are mingled with the liquid green of the Pines, makes a very gorgeous scene. Indeed, without the evergreens for contrast, the autumnal tints would lose much of their effect.

The Scarlet Oak asks a clear sky and the brightness of late October days. These bring out its colors. If the sun goes into a cloud, they become comparatively indistinct. As I sit on a cliff in the southwest part of our town, the sun is now getting low, and the woods in Lincoln, south and east of me, are lit up by its more level rays; and in the Scarlet Oaks, scattered so equally over the forest, there is brought out a more brilliant redness than I had believed was in them. Every tree of this species which is visible in those directions, even to the horizon, now stands out distinctly red. Some great ones lift their red backs high above the woods, in the next town, like huge roses with a myriad of fine petals; and some more slender ones, in a small grove of White Pines on Pine Hill in the east, on the

very verge of the horizon, alternating with the
Pines on the edge of the grove, and shoulder-
ing them with their red coats, look like sol-
diers in red amid hunters in green. This time
it is Lincoln green, too. Till the sun got low, I
did not believe that there were so many red
coats in the forest army. Theirs is an intense
burning red, which would lose some of its
strength, methinks, with every step you might
take toward them; for the shade that lurks
amid their foliage does not report itself at this
distance, and they are unanimously red. The
focus of their reflected color is in the atmosphere far on this side. Every such tree
becomes a nucleus of red, as it were, where,
with the declining sun, that color grows and
glows. It is partly borrowed fire, gathering
strength from the sun on its way to your eye.
It has only some comparatively dull red leaves
for a rallying-point, or kindling-stuff, to start
it, and it becomes an intense scarlet or red
mist, or fire, which finds fuel for itself in the
very atmosphere. So vivacious is redness. The
very rails reflect a rosy light at this hour and
season. You see a redder tree than exists.

If you wish to count the Scarlet Oaks, do it
now. In a clear day stand thus on a hill-top in

the woods, when the sun is an hour high, and every one within range of your vision, excepting in the west, will be revealed. You might live to the age of Methuselah and never find a tithe of them, otherwise. Yet sometimes even in a dark day I have thought them as bright as I ever saw them. Looking westward, their colors are lost in a blaze of light; but in other directions the whole forest is a flower-garden, in which these late roses burn, alternating with green, while the so-called "gardeners," walking here and there, perchance, beneath, with spade and water-pot, see only a few little asters amid withered leaves.

These are *my* China-asters, *my* late garden-flowers. It costs me nothing for a gardener. The falling leaves, all over the forest, are protecting the roots of my plants. Only look at what is to be seen, and you will have garden enough, without deepening the soil in your yard. We have only to elevate our view a little, to see the whole forest as a garden. The blossoming of the Scarlet Oak,—the forest-flower, surpassing all in splendor, (at least since the Maple)! I do not know but they interest me more than the Maples, they are so widely and equally dispersed throughout the forest; they are so hardy, a nobler tree on the whole;—our chief November flower, abiding the approach of winter with us, imparting warmth to early November prospects. It is remarkable that the latest bright color that is general should be this deep, dark scarlet and red, the intensest of colors. The ripest fruit of the year; like the cheek of a hard, glossy, red apple, from the cold Isle of Orleans, which will not be mellow for eating till next spring! When I rise to a hilltop, a thousand of these great Oak roses, distributed on every side, as far as the horizon! I admire them four or five miles off! This my unfailing prospect for a fortnight past! This late forest-flower surpasses all that spring or summer could do. Their colors were but rare and dainty specks comparatively, (created for the near-sighted, who walk amid the humblest herbs and underwoods,) and made no impression on a distant eye. Now it is an extended forest or a mountain-side, through or along which we journey from day to day, that bursts into bloom. Comparatively, our gardening is on a petty scale,—the gardener still nursing a few asters amid dead weeds, ignorant of the gigantic asters and roses, which, as it were, overshadow him, and ask for none of his care. It is like a little red paint ground on a saucer, and held up against the sunset sky. Why not take more elevated and broader views, walk in the great garden, not skulk in a little "debauched" nook of it? consider the beauty of the forest, and not merely of a few impounded herbs?

Let your walks now be a little more adventurous; ascend the hills. If, about the last of October, you ascend any hill in the outskirts of our town, and probably of yours, and look over the forest, you may see—well, what I have endeavored to describe. All this you surely *will* see, and much more, if you are prepared to see it,—if you *look* for it. Otherwise, regular and universal as this phenomenon is, whether you stand on the hill-top or in the hollow, you will think for threescore years and ten that all the wood is, at this season, sere and brown. Objects are concealed from our view, not so much because they are out of the course of our visual ray as because we do not bring our minds and eyes to bear on them; for there is no power to see in the eye itself, any more than in any other jelly. We do not realize how far and widely, or how near and narrowly, we are to look. The greater part of the phenomena of Nature are for this reason concealed from us all our lives. The gardener sees only the gardener's garden. Here, too, as in political economy, the supply answers to the demand. Nature does not cast pearls before swine. There is just as much beauty visible to us in the landscape as we are prepared to appreciate,—not a grain more. The actual objects which one man will see from a particular hilltop are just as different from those which another will see as the beholders are different. The Scarlet Oak must, in a sense, be in your eye when you go forth. We cannot see anything until we are possessed with the idea of it, take it into our heads,—and then we can hardly see anything else. In my botanical rambles, I find, that, first, the idea, or image, of a plant occupies my thoughts, though it may seem very foreign to this locality,—no nearer than Hudson's Bay,—and for some weeks or months I go thinking of it, and expecting it, unconsciously, and at length I surely see it. This is the history of my finding a score or more of rare plants, which I could name. A

man sees only what concerns him. A botanist
absorbed in the study of grasses does not distinguish the grandest Pasture Oaks. He, as
it were, tramples down Oaks unwittingly in
his walk, or at most sees only their shadows.
I have found that it required a different inten-
tion of the eye, in the same locality, to see
different plants, even when they were closely
allied, as *Juncaceæ* and *Gramineæ*: when I was
looking for the former, I did not see the latter
in the midst of them. How much more, then,
it requires different intentions of the eye and
of the mind to attend to different departments
of knowledge! How differently the poet and
the naturalist look at objects!

Take a New-England selectman, and set
him on the highest of our hills, and tell him to
look,—sharpening his sight to the utmost,
and putting on the glasses that suit him best,
(ay, using a spy-glass, if he likes,)—and make
a full report. What, probably, will he *spy*?—
what will he *select* to look at? Of course, he
will see a Brocken spectre of himself. He will
see several meeting-houses, at least, and, perhaps, that somebody ought to be assessed
higher than he is, since he has so handsome a

wood-lot. Now take Julius Cæsar, or Immanuel Swedenborg, or a Fegee-Islander, and set him up there. Or suppose all together, and let them compare notes afterward. Will it appear that they have enjoyed the same prospect? What they will see will be as different as Rome was from Heaven or Hell, or the last from the Fegee Islands. For aught we know, as strange a man as any of these is always at our elbow.

Why, it takes a sharp-shooter to bring down even such trivial game as snipes and woodcocks; he must take very particular aim, and know what he is aiming at. He would stand a very small chance, if he fired at random into the sky, being told that snipes were flying there. And so is it with him that shoots at beauty; though he wait till the sky falls, he will not bag any, if he does not already know its seasons and haunts, and the color of its wing,—if he has not dreamed of it, so that he can *anticipate* it; then, indeed, he flushes it at every step, shoots double and on the wing, with both barrels, even in cornfields. The sportsman trains himself, dresses and watches unweariedly, and loads and primes for his particular game. He prays for it, and offers sacrifices, and so he gets it. After due and long preparation, schooling his eye and hand, dreaming awake and asleep, with gun and paddle and boat he goes out after meadow-hens, which most of his townsmen never saw nor dreamed of, and paddles for miles against a head-wind, and wades in water up to his knees, being out all day without his dinner, and *therefore* he gets them. He had them half-way into his bag when he started, and has only to shove them down. The true sportsman can shoot you almost any of his game from his windows: what else has he windows or eyes for? It comes and perches at last on the barrel of his gun; but the rest of the world never see it *with the feathers on*. The geese fly exactly under his zenith, and honk when they get there, and he will keep himself supplied by firing up his chimney; twenty musquash have the refusal of each one of his traps before it is empty. If he lives, and his game-spirit increases, heaven and earth shall fail him sooner than game; and when he dies, he will go to more extensive, and, perchance, happier hunting-grounds. The fisherman, too, dreams of fish, sees a bobbing cork in his dreams, till he can almost catch them in his sink-spout. I knew a girl who, being sent to pick huckle-berries, picked wild gooseberries by the quart, where no one else knew that there were any, because she was accustomed to pick them up country where she came from. The astronomer knows where to go star-gathering, and sees one clearly in his mind before any have seen it with a glass. The hen scratches and finds her food right under where she stands; but such is not the way with the hawk.

These bright leaves which I have men-tioned are not the exception, but the rule; for I believe that all leaves, even grasses and mosses, acquire brighter colors just before their fall. When you come to observe faith-fully the changes of each humblest plant, you find that each has, sooner or later, its peculiar autumnal tint; and if you undertake to make a complete list of the bright tints, it will be nearly as long as a catalogue of the plants in your vicinity.

CPSIA information can be obtained at www.ICGtesting.com
Printed in the USA
LVOW091322171011

250851LV00001B/1/A